How To Handle Your Family Special

Scholastic Children's Books,
Commonwealth House, 1–19 New Oxford Street,
London WC1A 1NU, UK
a division of Scholastic Ltd
London ~ New York ~ Toronto ~ Sydney ~ Auckland
Mexico City ~ New Delhi ~ Hong Kong

First published in the UK by Scholastic Ltd, 2004

Text copyright © Roy Apps, 2004
Cover illustration copyright © Nick Sharratt, 2004
Inside illustrations copyright © Jo Moore, 2004

ISBN 0 439 96887 9

YOUR BROTHER

How To Handle Your Family Special

By Roy Apps

Illustrated by Jo Moore

Hippo

Contents

It was a dark and stormy night 7

Handling Super-Mums 15
  Quiz 1 16
  Quiz 2 24
  Quiz 3 29

Handling Super-Dads 34
  Quiz 4 35
  Quiz 5 43
  Quiz 6 49

Handling Super-Grans 52
  Quiz 7 53
  Quiz 8 54
  Quiz 9 62
  Quiz 10 66

Handling Super-Brothers 70
  Quiz 11 70
  Quiz 12 76
  Quiz 13 79

Handling Super-Sisters 85
  Quiz 14 85

Quiz 15 Part A 91
Quiz 15 Part B 95
Quiz 15 Part C 100

The How To Handle Your Family Dead
Important Family Factfinder File 105

The How To Handle Your Family Ultimate Quiz
Score Chart 107

The How To Handle Your Family Handler's
Certificate 110

It was a dark and stormy night...

and I was on holiday taking a well-earned break from my work writing books about how to handle all sorts of difficult people.* Suddenly, there was a ring at the door. Odd, I thought. Who would leave a ring at my door at this time of night? It wasn't as if I was getting engaged or anything.

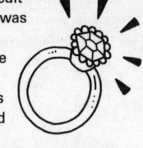

So I decided to open the door. I couldn't see a thing.

"Who's there?" I called.

"Sshhh!" came the reply.

Sshhh? Odd sort of name for a person, I thought. Then five figures appeared out of the darkness, holding their fingers to their lips: two girls and three boys.

* See *How To Handle your Mum/Dad, How To Handle Your Cat/Dog, How to Handle Your Teacher, How To Handle Your Gran* and *How To Handle Your Brother/Sister,* all available from Scholastic.

"Don't shout," the leader of the group whispered. "We don't want our parents to know we're here."

My heart was like the *Titanic* after it hit the iceberg: ie, sinking fast. I had a horrible feeling that these people were after my advice, even though I was on holiday.

"Look," I said, "can't you see the sign on my chalet? I've 'Dun Handling'."

"We know," said the leader of the group, a bossy sort of girl with a grin as wide as a shark's. "And now we think it's about time you dun some more."

"But I'm on holiday!" I protested. "And so are you. Surely you haven't got handling problems on holiday?"

"Look," said another of the gang, "unlike you we've all had to come on holiday WITH OUR FAMILIES."

"That's terrible," I said. "But I'm sorry, I really can't help you. Like I said, I'm on holiday. Nothing will make me change my mind."

"But you're the World's Number One Expert on handling your family!"

"I am?"

"Yes! You've got a brilliant and amazing brain for this sort of thing."

"I have?"

"Yes! You alone can save us from this hideous and horrible holiday-handling heartache!"

World's Number One Expert

"I can? Wait a minute! You won't change my mind by trying to flatter me," I said.

Suddenly, I was on the ground with three girls and two boys sitting on top of me.

"In that case we'll change your mind by trying to *flatten* you," said one of the boys.

"OK! I give up!" I replied. "You'd better come in."

Once inside my chalet, the leader of the pack said, "I'm Tamara, and these are my mates, Tanya, Talinder, Tony and Tom."

"Five 'T's?" I said.

"Make it five Cokes, if it's all the same with you," said Tamara. "None of us drink tea."

As they drank their Cokes, the five "T"s explained their family-handling problems to me.

"My mum won't let me wear my new crop top and miniskirt to the disco, even though I'm on holiday," complained Tamara.

I gasped in horror. "That is appalling!"

"My dad wants to take us on these boring trips, like fishing and stuff," sighed Tom.

"The heartless creature!" I agreed.

"And my brother's been grassing me up to our mum, telling her I've been sneaking out to meet some lads down the karaoke bar," said Tanya with a pout.

"Outrageous!" I replied.

"That's nothing. My sister's bagged the best bedroom in our chalet," muttered Talinder.

"How dare she!" I said.

"At least you haven't got your gran on holiday with you," said Tony. "She seems to think I should go to bed before midnight, even though we're on holiday!"

"Please stop!" I interrupted. "I can't bear to hear any more of these tortured tales of terrible treatment by members of your families!"

"Good. So you'll help us?" asked Tamara.

"I must," I said. "Because the fact that you're having problems with your mums, dads, brothers, sisters and grans is all my fault. You see, the *How To Handle* books have been falling into the wrong hands. They have been read by mums, dads, brothers, sisters and grans all over the world."

The five "T"s gasped in horror.

"And as a result," I explained, "a breed of Super-Mums, Super-Dads, Super-Brothers, Super-Sisters and Super-Grans have come into existence who are immune to all previously known handling techniques."

"You mean, a bit like Super-bugs and Super-rats?" said Tom.

I nodded.

A SUPER-BUG

A SUPER-MUM

A SUPER RAT

A SUPER-BROTHER

"What you need is an activity course, specially designed to help you acquire the skills needed to handle this new breed of

Super-Mums, Super-Dads, Super-Brothers, Super-Sisters and Super-Grans," I suggested.

"But where could we find such a course?" asked Talinder.

"Right here in the holiday park," I replied.

The five "T"s looked puzzled. Tamara had found a copy of the holiday brochure and was glancing through it. "There's nothing about a family-handling activity course in here," she said.

"Of course there isn't!" I exclaimed. "If there was, the first thing your mums, dads and grans would do would be to ban you all from signing up."

"Do you mean it's a *secret* activity course?" asked Tony.

"That's right," I said. "In fact, you're the only five people who know about it."*

"Wow," said Tanya.

"When does this secret family-handling activity course start?" asked Tom.

"When can you all get here?"

"First thing tomorrow?" suggested Tamara. "We're all down to do bungee jumping, go-kart racing and extreme mud wrestling, but this sounds much more useful!"

"I'll look forward to seeing you all then," I replied.

* Plus anyone who's reading this book, of course.

And so the very next morning...

I opened the door once again to Tamara, Tony, Tanya, Tom and Talinder.

"Before I can let you in," I whispered, "you must tell me what the secret password is."

Tamara shrugged. "Dunno," she said.

"Excellent!" I said. "*Dunno* is a very good choice of word for a secret password. I'll make sure I don't forget it. Come along in. The first part of the family-handling activity course is about to begin."

"Hang on," said Tony, "you haven't told us your name yet."

"My name is a secret, too," I told him.

"We've got to call you something. I know, perhaps we can call you an alias," suggested Tanya.

"You'd better not!" I replied. "Just call me The Quizmister."

"Don't you mean Quiz*master*?" said Talinder.

"Hey, I ask the questions around here," I said, firmly. "Now let's get down to business. The first part of the family-handling activity course is all about..."

Handling Super-Mums

"If you're going to become a skilled Super-Mum Handler," I explained, "it's vital for you to find out just what sort of mum you've got. So, when I was planning this activity course, I contacted the country's top psychologist and asked him if he would help me devise a special quiz about different sorts of mums."

"What did he say?" asked Tom.

"He said: 'On your bike!'" I replied.

"Weird," said Tom.

I nodded. "So I let him have a go on my bike. And while he was riding along on my bike, he devised the quiz below. I immediately realized my mistake: instead of contacting the country's top psychologist, I'd contacted the country's top bikologist."

TOP PSYCHOLOGIST

TOP BIKOLOGIST

Quiz 1: What Kind Of Mum Have You Got?

A quiz devised by the country's top bikologist.

Ask your mum the following simple questions. Her answers will reveal just what sort of mum she is:

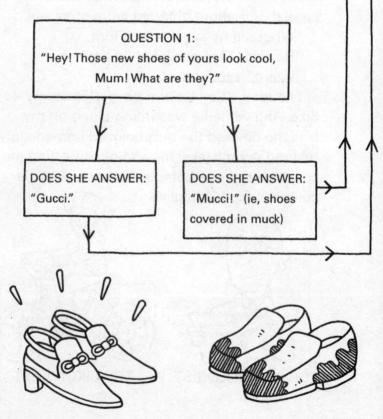

> QUESTION 1:
> "Hey! Those new shoes of yours look cool, Mum! What are they?"

DOES SHE ANSWER:
"Gucci."

DOES SHE ANSWER:
"Mucci!" (ie, shoes covered in muck)

YES!

YES!

WHAT HER ANSWER MEANS:
OK, your mum's got some sort of fashion sense. But hey, how come she can afford Gucci shoes when she's turned down your request for £150 a week pocket money?

WHAT HER ANSWER MEANS:
Your mum fancies herself as some sort of ageing hippy. Bad news.

Give her minus 20 points.

Give her minus 10 points and a pair of old wellies to wear: they'll be much-i less embarrassing than the Mucci shoes!

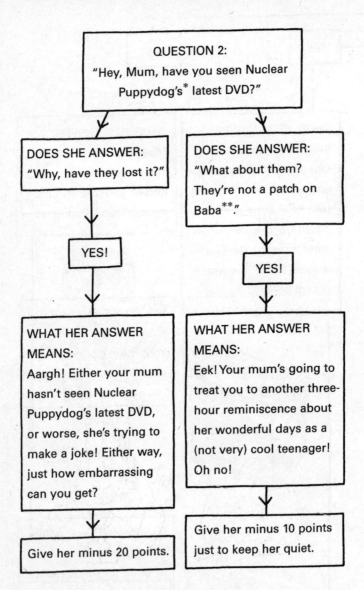

QUESTION 2:

"Hey, Mum, have you seen Nuclear Puppydog's* latest DVD?"

DOES SHE ANSWER:

"Why, have they lost it?"

YES!

WHAT HER ANSWER MEANS:

Aargh! Either your mum hasn't seen Nuclear Puppydog's latest DVD, or worse, she's trying to make a joke! Either way, just how embarrassing can you get?

Give her minus 20 points.

DOES SHE ANSWER:

"What about them? They're not a patch on Baba**."

YES!

WHAT HER ANSWER MEANS:

Eek! Your mum's going to treat you to another three-hour reminiscence about her wonderful days as a (not very) cool teenager! Oh no!

Give her minus 10 points just to keep her quiet.

* The number one coolest band of the lot!
** Baba, so called because they sounded like a load of old sheep, were your mum's fave band a hundred and fifty years ago when she was your age.

QUESTION 3:

"Do you like hip hop, Mum?"

DOES SHE ANSWER:

"Mmm, he's cute and cuddly!"

DOES SHE ANSWER:

"Hey, man! Is da well cool or wo?"

YES!

YES!

WHAT HER ANSWER MEANS:

Your mum thinks hip hop is a cuddly toy of the rabbit variety. How embarrassing!

WHAT HER ANSWER MEANS:

Your mum's pretending to be a hip hop fan. Aaargh! How excruciating!

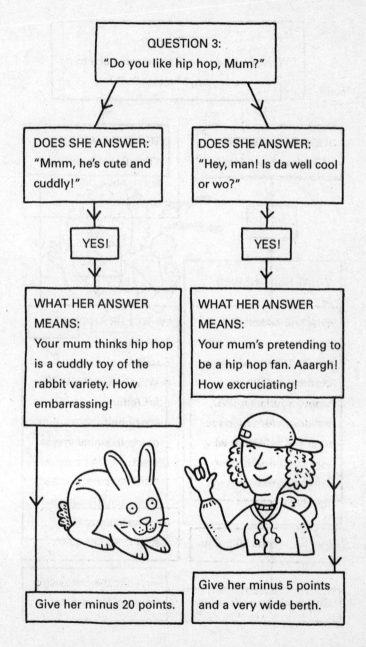

Give her minus 20 points.

Give her minus 5 points and a very wide berth.

QUESTION 4:

"Which TV show would you most like to be on, Mum?"

DOES SHE ANSWER: "Children From Hell."

DOES SHE ANSWER: "Pop Star Mums."

YES!

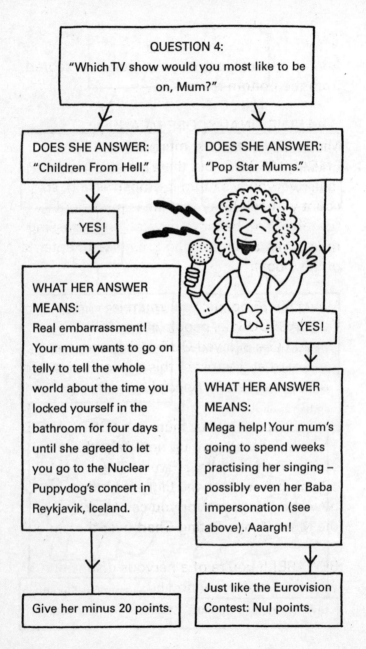

WHAT HER ANSWER MEANS:
Real embarrassment! Your mum wants to go on telly to tell the whole world about the time you locked yourself in the bathroom for four days until she agreed to let you go to the Nuclear Puppydog's concert in Reykjavik, Iceland.

YES!

WHAT HER ANSWER MEANS:
Mega help! Your mum's going to spend weeks practising her singing – possibly even her Baba impersonation (see above). Aaargh!

Give her minus 20 points.

Just like the Eurovision Contest: Nul points.

NOW:
Add up the total points your mum has scored
from the bottom rows.

WHAT THE FINAL SCORE MEANS:
Minus 80 points: Your mum is
EMBARRASSING, but there's nothing new in
that. Everybody's mum is embarrassing, so
count yourself lucky that life is just about
bearable. And better to have an embarrassing
mum, than an embracing gran (see Chapter 3
of this book).

Minus 30–75 points: Your mum is
OUTRAGEOUS: ie, people of her AGE
shouldn't be allowed OUT. Make sure you
work hard at the rest of this section in *How To
Handle Your Family Special*.

Minus 25 points: Your mum is a LOST CAUSE.
You may as well give up now. Take this copy
of *How To Handle Your Family Special* to
school and sell it to the highest bidder. Just
how bad things are for you can be seen on
the Mum Cringe-Rating Chart over the page.

BEWARE! If you're of a nervous disposition,
you must look away now!
   I said now!

MUM CRINGE-RATING CHART

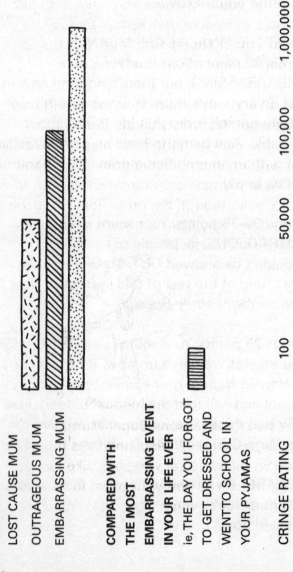

FACTOR
LOST CAUSE MUM
OUTRAGEOUS MUM
EMBARRASSING MUM

COMPARED WITH
THE MOST
EMBARRASSING EVENT
IN YOUR LIFE EVER
ie, THE DAY YOU FORGOT
TO GET DRESSED AND
WENT TO SCHOOL IN
YOUR PYJAMAS

CRINGE RATING

1,000,000

100,000

50,000

100

Now enter your mum's score from Quiz 1, together with the name of the type of mum you now know you have, on your How To Handle Your Family Dead Important Family Factfinder File on page 105 at the back of this book.

"It's all very well knowing what sort of mum you've got, Quizmister," said Tamara, "but how do I deal with the particular problem I've got with my mum? Remember? She won't let me wear my new crop top and miniskirt to the disco, even though I'm on holiday? And when I asked her why, she said she'd seen better-dressed scarecrows!"

"One of the reasons Super-Mums are so difficult to handle," I explained, "is that they have so many secret weapons, like Lippy-Stick, which enabled your mum to make that lippy remark to you. But don't worry. Help is at hand when you do…"

Quiz 2: Finding Your Super-Mum's Secret Weapons

See if you can match your Super-Mum's secret weapons to the part of her head where they are most likely to be found.

SUPER-MUM'S SECRET WEAPONS
(Write the correct secret weapon next to the appropriate letter on the correct part of your mum's head on page 25.)

HOW TO SCORE: Take 10 points for every correct answer and minus 10 points for every incorrect answer.

1. MASCAR-Y:
Stuff she puts round her **** to make them really scary, so that when you want to ask her a perfectly reasonable question, like

Can I buy a DVD of Revenge of the Killer Mutant Vampire Werewolf III, Mum?

you get all tongue-tied.

YOUR MUM:

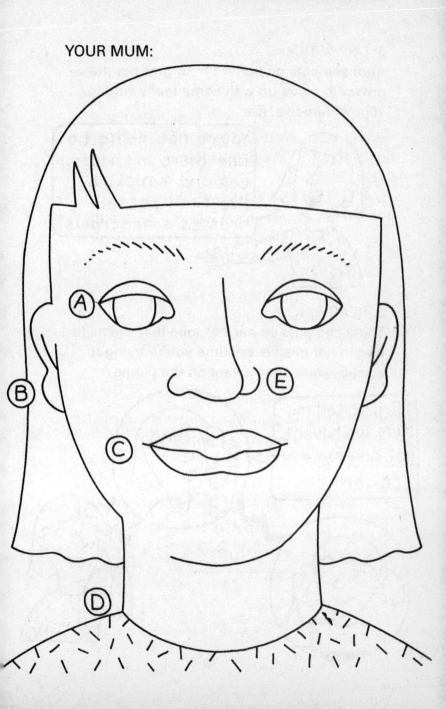

2. LIPPY-STICK:

Stuff she puts on her ***** to give her the power to come up with some really cutting, "lippy" remarks, like

You're not going to the disco in that crop top and miniskirt? I've seen better-dressed scarecrows!

3. HEAR RING:

Thing she puts on her *** lobe that seems to ring in her head every time you're trying to discuss something secret on the phone.

I'll just tell my mum we haven't got any homework tonight!

4. NOSEY STUD:
Goes on her **** to sniff out anything remotely fishy.

5. GET-IT-IN-THE-NECK LACE:
Thing she wears around her **** that contains a miniature infra-red camera that spots you doing things she doesn't approve of.

ANSWERS:
A = 1. MASCAR-Y

B = 3. HEAR RING

C = 2. LIPPY-STICK

D = 5. GET-IT-IN-THE-NECK LACE

E = 4. NOSEY STUD

HOW DID YOU SCORE?
50 points: Brilliant! Now you can be really
on your guard against your mum's secret
weapons.

20–40 points: Could do better! In fact, a slug
with the brain of a jellyfish could probably
do better.[*]

Less than 20 points: Pathetic! Super-Mum
handler? You're not even on the way to
becoming a Super-*dumb* handler.[**]

> *Now enter your score from Quiz 2 on
> your How To Handle Your Family
> Ultimate Quiz Score Chart on page 107
> at the back of the book.*

[*] Typical Super-Mum Lippy-Stick comment.
[**] Another typical Super-Mum Lippy-Stick comment.

"That's great, Quizmister," said Tamara, "but how can we get our own back against our Super-Mums?"

"What you need," I suggested, "is a special word you can call your mum when you're cross with her without her telling you to watch your language."

"Exactly!" said Tamara.

"Hmmm, I don't think calling your mum 'Exactly' would help you get your own back on her," I said. "But, don't worry, for after months of painstaking research I have devised a word that will. And to find out what it is, all you have to do is..."

Quiz 3: Discover The How To Handle Your Family Super-Mum Crossword

Complete the answers to the following seven clues, which are all to do with mum handling. The missing letters will spell a word you can call your mum when you're cross, without *her* telling *you* to watch your language.

CLUES:

1. You might say this if your mum catches you with her "Get-It-In-The-Neck Lace".

__hat me, Mum?

2. You might say this if your mum catches you out with her Nosey Stud.

__oo-er!

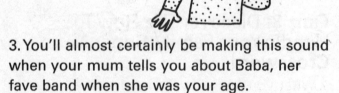

3. You'll almost certainly be making this sound when your mum tells you about Baba, her fave band when she was your age.

__zzzzzzzzzzzzz...

4. Your mum's *still* rabbitting on about Baba, so you're still making this sound.

_zzzzzzzzzzzzzz...

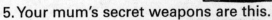

5. Your mum's secret weapons are this.

_ethal.

6. You might say this if your mum catches you out with her Hear Ring.

_eekkkkkkkk!

7. What *you* think of your mum's fave group Baba.

_ ubbish!

ANSWERS:

1. **W** hat me, Mum?
2. **O** oo-er!
3. **Z** zzzzzzzzzzzzzz...
4. **Z** zzzzzzzzzzzzzz...
5. **L** ethal.
6. **E** eekkkkkkkk!
7. **R** ubbish!

Yes, WOZZLER is the word, as in, "Oh, Mum, don't be such a wozzler!"

AMAZING FAMILY FACTFINDER FACT:
a wozzler is someone who thinks that something that <u>wozz</u> cool about three months ago, is still cool now. As in:

These cut-off jeans are so cool, don't you think?

Oh, Mum, you really are a wozzler!

Now enter this brilliant word on your How To Handle Your Family Dead Important Family Factfinder File on page 105 at the back of the book.

"That's brilliant, Quizmister," said Tamara.

"Yes, it is rather, isn't it?" I agreed, modestly.

"I think it's completely useless," said Tom, sulkily. "Some of us aren't on holiday with our mums, we're on holiday with our dads."

"Becoming a Super-Dad Handler is no different to becoming a Super-Mum Handler," I explained. "First of all you've got to find out just what sort of dad you've got."

"And how do we do that?" asked Tom.

"By stopping sulking and paying attention to the next part of the activity course," I replied. "Which is all about..."

Handling Super-Dads

"What about me?" asked Tanya.

"What about you?" I enquired.

"I've got a step-dad."

"Step-dads need handling in just the same way," I said. "But first, a word of warning."

BEWARE

"And now, another word of warning: step-dads are not to be confused with step-ladder dads. These are dads who spend all their time up step-ladders. Of course, they claim they're doing DIY, but really they're spying on you and your mates having a bit of perfectly harmless fun."

What do you think you're doing, stuffing my prize tomatoes into your Super-Blast water pistol?

"Anyway, I asked a top psychologist to help me devise a quiz that would enable people to find out just what sort of dad they'd got."

"And what did he say this time?" asked Tom.

"Pah!" I replied. "To which I answered, I don't care whether you call your dad pah, pop, daddy, father or old baldytop, would you help me devise this quiz, please?"

"The top psychologist gave a big sigh – and that was when I realized he wasn't a top psychologist at all, more a *sigh*-cologist."

"Very well then," he agreed, "if you insist."

Quiz 4: What Kind Of Dad Have You Got?

Study your dad's lifestyle. Then answer the following questions about his behaviour:

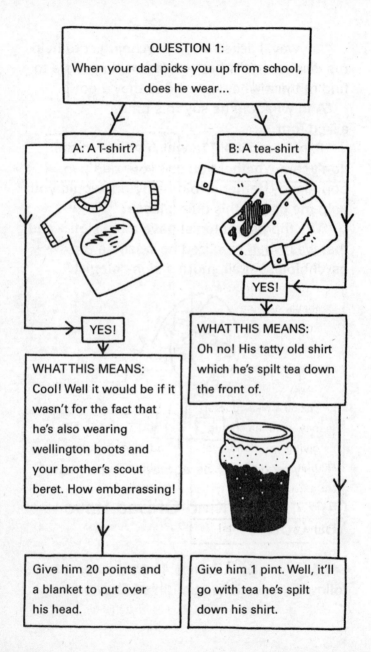

QUESTION 1:

When your dad picks you up from school, does he wear...

A: A T-shirt?

B: A tea-shirt

YES!

YES!

WHAT THIS MEANS:
Cool! Well it would be if it wasn't for the fact that he's also wearing wellington boots and your brother's scout beret. How embarrassing!

WHAT THIS MEANS:
Oh no! His tatty old shirt which he's spilt tea down the front of.

Give him 20 points and a blanket to put over his head.

Give him 1 pint. Well, it'll go with tea he's spilt down his shirt.

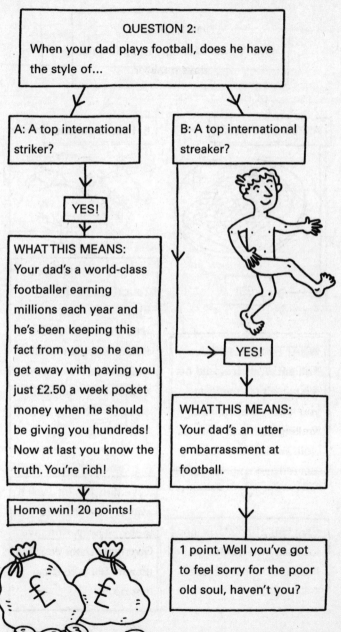

QUESTION 2:

When your dad plays football, does he have the style of...

A: A top international striker?

B: A top international streaker?

YES!

WHAT THIS MEANS:
Your dad's a world-class footballer earning millions each year and he's been keeping this fact from you so he can get away with paying you just £2.50 a week pocket money when he should be giving you hundreds! Now at last you know the truth. You're rich!

Home win! 20 points!

YES!

WHAT THIS MEANS:
Your dad's an utter embarrassment at football.

1 point. Well you've got to feel sorry for the poor old soul, haven't you?

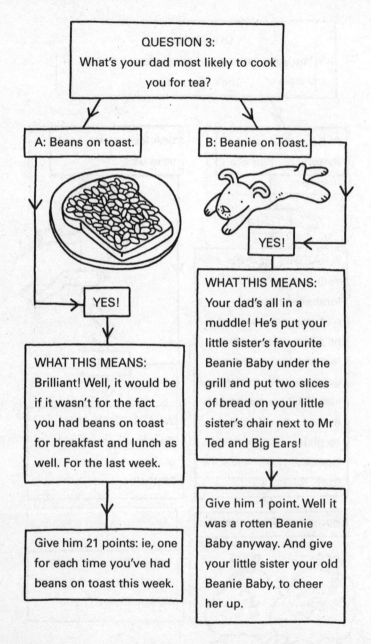

QUESTION 3:

What's your dad most likely to cook you for tea?

A: Beans on toast.

B: Beanie on Toast.

YES!

YES!

WHAT THIS MEANS:
Brilliant! Well, it would be if it wasn't for the fact you had beans on toast for breakfast and lunch as well. For the last week.

WHAT THIS MEANS:
Your dad's all in a muddle! He's put your little sister's favourite Beanie Baby under the grill and put two slices of bread on your little sister's chair next to Mr Ted and Big Ears!

Give him 21 points: ie, one for each time you've had beans on toast this week.

Give him 1 point. Well it was a rotten Beanie Baby anyway. And give your little sister your old Beanie Baby, to cheer her up.

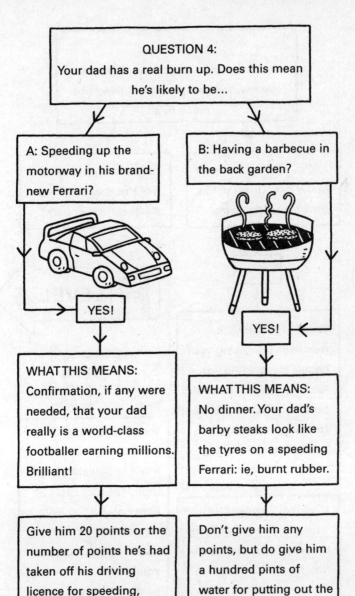

QUESTION 4:
Your dad has a real burn up. Does this mean he's likely to be...

A: Speeding up the motorway in his brand-new Ferrari?

B: Having a barbecue in the back garden?

YES!

YES!

WHAT THIS MEANS:
Confirmation, if any were needed, that your dad really is a world-class footballer earning millions. Brilliant!

WHAT THIS MEANS:
No dinner. Your dad's barby steaks look like the tyres on a speeding Ferrari: ie, burnt rubber.

Give him 20 points or the number of points he's had taken off his driving licence for speeding, whichever is the greater.

Don't give him any points, but do give him a hundred pints of water for putting out the barby steaks.

QUESTION 5:
Your dad comes in and says, "Wha-hay! I've reached Level 5 today!" Does this mean he's...

A: Got to Level 5 of your brand-new Quest of the Dork computer game

B: Found his way to Level 5 of the shopping centre multi-storey car park?

YES!

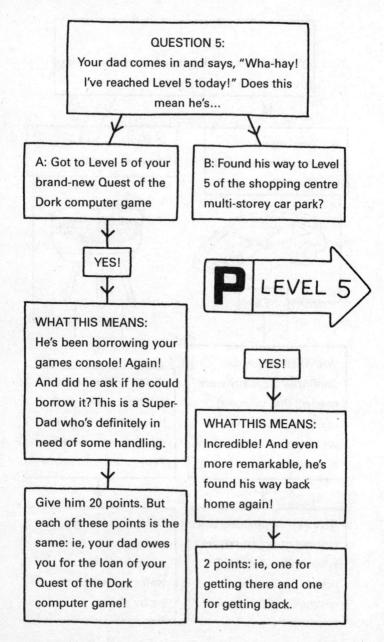

WHAT THIS MEANS:
He's been borrowing your games console! Again! And did he ask if he could borrow it? This is a Super-Dad who's definitely in need of some handling.

Give him 20 points. But each of these points is the same: ie, your dad owes you for the loan of your Quest of the Dork computer game!

YES!

WHAT THIS MEANS:
Incredible! And even more remarkable, he's found his way back home again!

2 points: ie, one for getting there and one for getting back.

NOW:
Add up the total points your dad has scored from the bottom rows.

WHAT THE FINAL SCORE MEANS:

101 points: Your dad is a HOPELESS CASE. Hey, there's no need to feel sorry for yourself, because where dads are concerned this is about as good as it gets. You're one of the lucky ones. In fact, you may be the *only* lucky one.

60–100 points: Your dad is a HELPLESS CASE. Not that I expect you were ever thinking of helping him, anyway, were you? If you were, don't bother. Find something easier to do, like scratching your head with your big toe.

Less than 60 points: Your dad is a complete and utter BASKET CASE.

And if your dad is one of those dads who is always getting lost down the cooked-meats aisle in the supermarket, he's likely to be a SHOPPING-BASKET CASE as well.

*Now enter your dad's score from Quiz 4
together with the name of the type of
dad you now know you have, on your
How To Handle Your Family Dead
Important Family Factfinder File on
page 105 at the back of this book.*

Tom looked well pleased. "Thanks,
Quizmister," he said, "but can you help me
with the particular Super-Dad problem I told
you about?"

"I've forgotten what it was. It was quite a
long time ago when you first mentioned it,"
I said.*

"It's just that my dad wants to take us on
these boring trips, like fishing and stuff,"
sighed Tom.

"In other words," I said, "you're being taken
for a ride. You see, when dads say something,
they always *mean* something completely
different. But don't worry. Help is at hand in
the form of..."

*32 pages ago to be precise.

Quiz 5: Learning Super-Dad-Speak

Test yourself on these common dad sayings and in each case see if you can work out what he really means, ie, which saying is so *cool* and which one is so *cruel*. Is it A or B? Put a circle round the one *you* think your dad really means:

1. YOU *HEAR* YOUR DAD SAY:

"I thought we'd spend the day by the water."

WHAT DOES THIS *REALLY* MEAN IN SUPER-DAD-SPEAK?

A) He's taking you for a fun-packed day at the local beach?

OR

B) He's taking you fishing?

2. YOU *HEAR* YOUR DAD SAY:

"How about coming
to see if we can get
a bite?"*

WHAT DOES THIS *REALLY* MEAN IN SUPER-DAD-SPEAK?

A) He's taking you for a
slap-up meal at the local
burger bar?

OR

B) He's taking you fishing
again?

3. YOU *HEAR* YOUR DAD SAY:

"Let's go and see if you'll
get a really good filling
this time."

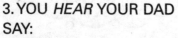

* Of course, if it's midnight and there's a full moon when your dad says this, it probably means he's a vampire.

WHAT DOES THIS *REALLY* MEAN IN SUPER-DAD-SPEAK?

A) He's taking you up to the counter to get *another* burger to put in your bun – this time one with extra cheese and BBQ sauce?

OR

B) He's taking you to the dentist?

4. YOU *HEAR* YOUR DAD SAY:

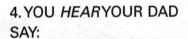

"I thought we'd spend the morning on the net."

WHAT DOES THIS
REALLY MEAN IN
SUPER-DAD-SPEAK?

A) He's taking you to the
local cyber café?

OR

B) You've got to help
mend his fishing tackle?

5. YOU *HEAR* YOUR DAD SAY:

"Hey! What a perfect day
for a sail!"

WHAT DOES THIS
REALLY MEAN IN
SUPER-DAD-SPEAK?

A) You're going
on a fab trip
round the bay in
a luxury yacht?

OR

B) He actually means "a perfect day for a *sale*" and you've got to spend the morning going round the local boot sales looking for bargain fishing tackle?

6. YOU *HEAR* YOUR DAD SAY:

"I thought we'd find a nice place for a picnic."

WHAT DOES THIS *REALLY* MEAN IN SUPER-DAD-SPEAK?

A) You're going for a walk in the woods or on the beach to look for a cool picnic spot?

OR

B) He's really intending to find a nice *plaice* for a picnic: ie, fishing yet again!

ANSWERS:
In each question B is the right answer and the example of what your dad really means. Take one point for every correct answer:

HOW DID YOU SCORE?
6 points: Well done! You've got your dad's Super-Dad-Speak to a state where it's just like a half-eaten lolly: ie, well and truly licked.

3–5 points: Not bad! You're well on the way there: there being one of your dad's boring fishing trips. So, why not demand he turns the car round and drives you home while you've still got the chance?

0–2 points: Hmmm. You still need a bit of work on this one. Why not go through this section again. And again. After all, you'll have plenty of time while you sit around on all those fishing trips.

Now enter your score from Quiz 5 on your How To Handle your Family Ultimate Quiz Score Chart on page 107 at the back of the book.

"Yeah, that's well cool, Quizmister," said Tom, happily smiling now. "But it'd be even more well cool to be able to turn the tables on my Super-Dad."

"No probs," I replied. "Just pick up the corner of the dining-room table, preferably while it's still loaded with plates, and turn it up in the direction of your dad."

Tom frowned. "I don't think so, somehow," he said.

"OK," I agreed. "Then why not do..."

Quiz 6: Discover Your Very Own Super-Dad-Speak Phrase

Fill in the answers to the following questions to discover a phrase that will mean one thing to your dad – but quite another to you!

1. Your dad might well say, "You will love fishing." To which you might reply, "Oh no, I...
__ __ __ 'T

2. After your dad has sat down on the box of fishing hooks you placed on his seat, his bottom is likely to be very... TEN __ __ __

3. Going fishing with your dad is so boring it could well damage your brilliant...

— — — — —

And the Super-Dad-Speak phrase is...........

ANSWER: WON-DER BRAIN

And this is how it works. Your dad has said something particularly daft in Super-Dad-Speak: eg, "I thought we'd spend the day by the water, to see if we can get a bite of something like a nice plaice for a picnic." In other words, go fishing.

YOU SAY: "Oh, Dad, you're wonder brain!"

YOUR DAD *HEARS* YOU SAY:

"Oh, Dad, you're Wonder Brain!"

(ie, he thinks Wonder Brain is the latest super hero, of course.)

BUT WHAT YOU <u>REALLY</u> MEAN IN DAD-
SPEAK, IS:

"Oh, Dad, you're one
der brain!"

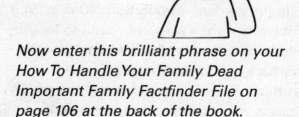

Now enter this brilliant phrase on your
How To Handle Your Family Dead
Important Family Factfinder File on
page 106 at the back of the book.

"Thanks, Quizmister, that's so cool," said Tom.

I shrugged, modestly. "Sensational
solutions, amazing answers, mind-boggling
masterplans, they're all part of the Quizmister
family-handling course."

"Huh! Quizmister? *Swiz*mister more like,"
muttered Tony, darkly. "I haven't come on
holiday with my mum or my dad. I've come
with my gran!"

"Hey, no probs, Tony," I told him. "We'll
now do a bit of..."

Handling Super-Grans

"Take me to your gran," I said. "And I'll show you how to handle her. Where is she?"

"In the garden," said Tony.

However, when we went round to Tony's holiday chalet, we couldn't see his gran anywhere. In fact, all we could see was this:

Quiz 7: Where's Granny?

There are six things we saw in the garden that could've been Tony's gran, but only one of the things actually *was* her. The other things in the garden were a scarecrow, a garden gnome, a statue, a gargoyle and a Hallowe'en pumpkin.

Mark the scarecrow, garden gnome, statue, gargoyle and Hallowe'en pumpkin with an X. Don't, whatever you do, mark Tony's gran with a X: she'll only want a sloppy X back.

HOW TO SCORE: Score one point each for finding the scarecrow, garden gnome, statue, gargoyle and Hallowe'en pumpkin. Score 100 points for finding Tony's gran.

> *Now enter your score from Quiz 7 on your How To Handle your Family Ultimate Quiz Score Chart on page 107 at the back of the book.*

"Why is your gran hiding?" I asked Tony.

"She's afraid I've come to ask her to baby-sit Tanya's little brother," Tony replied.

"Is Tanya's little brother that bad?" I asked.

"No, he's worse," said Tanya.

Anyway, once we'd found Tony's gran, I was able to set everyone to work on...

Quiz 8: Can You Complete The Super-Gran Timeline?

A Super-Gran Timeline is just like carbon dating; except you don't need a degree in chemistry to be able to do it, you don't need any complex, scientific data-handling equipment and you don't need any carbon. OK, it's actually not like carbon dating at all. In fact, all you have to do is get your gran to help you put the following events in the correct place on the timeline at the bottom of the page.

1. THE YEAR: THE ICE AGE BEGAN

2. THE YEAR: YOUR GRAN WAS BORN

3. THE YEAR: THE BATTLE OF HASTINGS TOOK PLACE

4. THE YEAR: YOUR GRAN'S CAR WAS MADE

1.000.000 BC | 1000 | 1100 | 1200 | 1300 | 1400

5. THE YEAR: ENGLAND WON THE WORLD CUP

6. THE YEAR: YOUR GRAN STARTED TO KNIT THE JUMPER SHE GAVE YOU LAST CHRISTMAS

7. THE YEAR: YOUR MUM'S FAVE BAND BABA LAST HAD A RECORD IN THE CHARTS

8. THE YEAR: YOUR GRAN STARTED TO KNIT THE JUMPER SHE'S GOING TO GIVE YOU FOR NEXT CHRISTMAS

9. THE YEAR: KENTUCKY FRIED DODO WENT BUST

10. THE YEAR: OF THE GUM-POWDER PLOT (ie, the year your dad mixed curry powder in your gran's toothpaste in a bid to stop her talking)

| | | | | | | |
|1500|1600|1700|1800|1900|2000|2100|

HOW TO WORK OUT WHAT TYPE OF GRAN
YOU'VE GOT:
Are ALL the events on the timeline featuring
your gran dated BEFORE 1100?

YES?

WHAT TYPE OF GRAN YOU'VE GOT:

PRACTICALLY PREHISTORIC

WHAT THIS MEANS FOR YOU: COOL NEWS!
The BBC are likely to want to follow up their
Walking With Dinosaurs and *Walking With
Cavemen* series with *Walking With Practically
Prehistoric Grans.* Play your cards right and
you could become a TV star!

Are MORE THAN THREE of the events on the timeline featuring your gran dated BEFORE 1100?

YES?

WHAT TYPE OF GRAN YOU'VE GOT:

SIMPLY ANCIENT

WHAT THIS MEANS FOR YOU: COOL NEWS *again*! Because your gran is so ancient, you can turn her into an Ancient Historical Tourist attraction. Coach loads of tourists will pay you (yes, *pay* you!) large sums of money to be shown round your gran. Untold riches will soon be yours!

Are LESS THAN THREE of the events on the timeline featuring your gran dated BEFORE 1100?

YES?

WHAT TYPE OF GRAN YOU'VE GOT:

GETTING ON

WHAT THIS MEANS FOR YOU: BAD NEWS! Because these are some of the things your gran will be getting on:
1. GETTING ON to your mum about the state of your bedroom.

2. GETTING ON her high horse about how easy children have it at school these days.

In short:

3. GETTING ON your nerves.

HOWEVER!!!!!! If NONE of the events on the timeline featuring your gran are dated BEFORE 1100, then your gran is telling porkies.

WHAT THIS MEANS FOR YOU: You STILL need to find out how old your gran really is. You could use one of the following instruments of torture:
1. THE RACK – wait till your gran is dozing in front of the telly, then pick your brother's loudest Squidgy Bogies CD from the *CD Rack*. Put it on and don't turn it off until your gran comes clean about her age.

OR If your brother hasn't got a Squidgy Bogies CD...

2. THE THUMB SCREWS – wait till your gran is dozing in front of the telly then wet your thumb thoroughly and rub it down the window. It'll make an excruciating sound (though not as excruciating as the Squidgy Bogies). Don't stop until your gran tells you her true age.

OR You can simply ask your gran some trick historical questions: ie,

3. THE
INQUISITION:

YOU: Gran, tell us about the holidays you had when you were a girl.
GRAN: We always used to go down to Hastings, though one year we couldn't.
YOU: Why not, Gran?
GRAN: There was this battle on.

There! Your gran's let slip that she was around in 1066, just as you always suspected!

Now enter the the name of the type of gran you've got on your How To Handle Your Family Dead Important Family Factfinder File on page 106 at the back of this book.

"That's great news about the possible telly series," said Tony, "but it still doesn't solve the problem that my gran thinks I should go to bed before midnight, even though we're on holiday!"

"No, the Gran Timeline doesn't solve that problem," I agreed. "But the Bored Game does."

"Did you say Board Game?" asked Talinder.

"No," I replied. "I said Bored Game. The Bored Game is a game that will bore your gran so much she'll fall asleep instantly, leaving you free to stay up as late as you want!"

"Wow! How do we learn to play?" asked Tony, eagerly.

"How do you think?" I replied. "All you have to do is..."

Quiz 9: Learning To Play The Bored Game

The BORED GAME consists of a series of really tricky and difficult questions for which points are given for the correct answers.

HOW TO SCORE: 10 points for every right answer

QUESTIONS:

1. DESIGN TECHNOLOGY
How do you make a bandstand?

2. WILDLIFE
Name three members of the skunk family

3. ASTRONOMY
What planet is older than Mars?

4. GEOGRAPHY
What is the capital of France?

5. SEA LIFE
Where would you go to find a man-eating fish?

6. LITERATURE
Why have elephants got Big Ears?

7. THE LAW
What did the police officer say to his stomach?

8. THE ANIMAL KINGDOM
What was the famous dog called who was so clever he could say his own name?

9. HISTORY
Why did they bury Henry the Fifth at Westminster Abbey?

10. FOOD TECH
How do you make an egg roll?

ANSWERS:
1. Nick their chairs.
2. Daddy Skunk; Mummy Skunk; Baby Skunk.
3. Gran Mars.
4. F.
5. A seafood restaurant.
6. Noddy won't pay the ransom.
7. You're under a vest.
8. Woof woof.
9. Because he was dead.
10. Push it down a hill.

HOW DID YOU DO?
100 points: Excellent. You're obviously an UTTER BORE.

50–100 points: How you didn't manage to get all the questions right, I don't know. You're not so much an UTTER BORE as a NUTTER BORE.

Less than 50 points: Useless. You completely misunderstood the questions. I bet that's made you really mad. If it has, you could well turn into a WILD BORE. Check the pictures below to find out.

Now enter your score from Quiz 9 on your How To Handle Your Family Ultimate Quiz Score Chart on page 107 at the back of the book.

"Of course," I explained, "making you go to bed before midnight isn't the only appalling thing that grans like to do. They also like giving you things."

"That's good, isn't it?" asked Tamara.

I shook my head. "No. The sort of things grans like giving you aren't things you enjoy getting."

"Have you got any examples?" asked Tamara.

I nodded. "However, they're not the sort of things I like to talk about in public so I usually refer to them by using anagrans."

"What's an anagran?" asked Tony.

"Have you ever heard of *anagrams*? They're words made up by rearranging the letters of another word. Like..."

ATE is an anagram of TEA

And

NERKLOP is an anagram of PLONKER

"*Anagrans* are words made up by rearranging the letters into other words, which describe some of the terrifying things a gran likes to give you."

"Have you got any examples?" asked Tom.

"Yes," I replied. "There are seven here in..."

Quiz 10: Test Your Skill With These ANAGRANS!

Can you rearrange the letters in the following words to make ANAGRANS?

HOW TO SCORE: Put a football in front of your feet and take aim at the goal.

HOW TO SCORE IN THE ANAGRAN QUIZ:
Take 10 points for each correct answer.

WORDS → ↓   ANAGRAN
REARRANGE TO MAKE →

1. OPPSY SIKSES _____

2. LOPPSY SIKSES _____

3. GIB GUH _____

4. NOTHERA GIB GUH _____

5. TOLS FO LEDDUCS _____

6. LOOLWY BLOBBE AHT _____

7. BEEVTALEGS _____

ANSWERS:
The things grans like to give you are:
1. Soppy kisses; 2. Sloppy kisses; 3. Big hug;
4. Another big hug; 5. Lots of cuddles; 6.
Woolly bobble hat; 7. Vegetables.

HOW DID YOU DO?
70 points: Llew enod! You're a rats!

40–70 points: Ton dab. But don't blame me if
your gran gives you a silly loolwy blobbe aht
for Christmas.

Less than 40 points. You really are a lawly
brian!

> *Now enter your score from Quiz 10 on*
> *your How To Handle Your Family*
> *Ultimate Quiz Score Chart on page 107*
> *at the back of the book.*

"Thanks, Quizmister," said Tony. "That's really
helpful."

"But not as helpful as the stuff he's going
to tell us about handling Super-Brothers," said
Tanya.

"You reckon he can teach you to handle
your little brother? You must be joking,"
laughed Tony.

"I'd *never* joke about my brother," said Tanya. "He's no laughing matter." She paused for a moment. "Unless he's standing on the fireplace with his head stuck up the chimney."

"Finding out what kind of brother you've got can be like setting off a smoke detector," I pointed out.

Tanya looked puzzled. "What do you mean?" she asked.

"I mean it can be a really *alarming* experience," I explained.

"We can take it, can't we, guys?" Tanya asked her mates.

They all nodded.

"We've all got Super-Brothers, too," Talinder said. "And we're desperate to find out how to handle them."

"Then it's time," I said, "for..."

Handling Super-Brothers

Quiz 11: What Sort Of Super-Bruv Have You Got?

Put a ring around the answers which best describe what your brother's like:

QUESTIONS:

ANSWERS:

1. What is your brother most likely to have perched on top of his head?

A) A pair of Calvin Klein shades
B) A pair of Calvin Klein underpants
C) Two pairs of Calvin Klein underpants

2. What are your brother's fave hobbies?

A) Sky diving
B) Sky watching
C) Skiving

3. What is your brother's fave sport?

A) Gran Prix motor racing
B) Power-boat racing
C) Slug racing

4. Which of these foods best describes your brother?

A) A small bowl of spaghetti
B) A fruitcake
C) A Pot Noodle

5. Who has the creepiest leer?

A) Count Dracula
B) Draco Malfoy
C) Your brother

Now tot up the scores like this:

1. A) 5 points – Cool! Well it would be if it wasn't the middle of winter and your brother was also wearing a multicoloured bobble hat.*
B) 10 points – your brother's not so much cool as freezing.

* ie, the one knitted by your gran (see above).

C) 2 points – one for each pair of pants.

2. A) 5 points – Cool again! Well it would be if it wasn't for the fact that your brother has confused sky diving with scuba diving and is drifting merrily through the clouds wearing a wetsuit.

B) 10 points – this is *soo* annoying. It means you never get to watch telly!

C) 100 points – this is *sooooooooo* annoying. He skives out of doing his share of horrible household jobs: eg, loading the dishwasher, feeding the dog, kissing the granny (see pages 52 to 68). No wonder you don't have time to do it all before going out with your mates and end up getting the dog to kiss granny before you load her into the dishwasher with a bowl of dog food.

3. A) 5 points – Hot sport or what! Well it would be if it was Grand Prix motor racing instead of *Gran* Prix racing: ie, your brother's lined up your gran and her friends, just to see which one can run the furthest.

B) 10 points – this would be cool, but unfortunately your brother does his power-boat racing in the bath.

C) 100 points – it's sooooooo hard to tell which one's the slug and which one's your brother.

4. A) 5 points – A small bowl of spaghetti is a LITTLE PASTA. Your brother is a LITTLE PESTA.

B) 10 points – yep, most brothers are FRUITCAKES – of the particularly nutty variety.

C) 100 points – was a more accurate term for brothers ever invented?

5. A) 0 points – I mean, come on, Count Drac can only look creepy during the hours of darkness for one night in the month only. Is that pathetic or what?

B) 0 points – Draco Malfoy's just a character in a book, which your brother isn't. More's the pity.

C) 100 points! Eat your heart out, Count Dracula! No, I didn't mean literally.

WHAT THE SCORES MEAN:
If your brother has scored up to 30 points, he's just a BIT OF A JOKE.

30–100 points: He's A BAD JOKE.

Over 100 points: He's SIMPLY PAST A JOKE.

> *Now enter your brother's score from Quiz 11, together with the name of the type of brother you now know you have, on your How To Handle Your Family Dead Important Family Factfinder File on page 106 at the back of this book.*

"OK, Quizmister," said Tanya, "so it's officially confirmed, my brother's simply past a joke. But how am I going to stop him grassing me up to our mum? I mean, he's actually been telling her I've been sneaking out of the chalet to meet some lads down the karaoke bar."

"That's terrible, Tanya," I agreed.

"You're telling me," said Tanya. "I'd *never* sneak out to meet some lads down the karaoke bar. That would be so gross! No, I'd meet them all down by the swimming pool."

"The best way to stop your Super-Brother sneaking on you is to make sure his lips are sealed," I said.

"And how do I do that?" asked Tanya.

"With a bag of How to Handle Your Family toffee. This is like ordinary toffee, except it has a special SECRET ingredient," I explained. "Now, it's no use just *giving* your brother a bag of toffees. He'd only say, "Why are you giving me these toffees? What's wrong with them?" Brothers have these really suspicious minds, you see. Sad, but that's the way it is."

Tanya nodded.

"What you need to do," I continued, "is to leave the bag of toffees lying about, so that he'll just help himself."*

"So what is this secret ingredient?" asked Tanya.

* You can make sure he tries the toffees by sticking the kind of label on the bag that you know will appeal to him. You'll find a suitable label on page 77. Colour it in, if you like, to make it more realistic.

"I could just tell you what the secret ingredient is, I suppose," I replied, "but to make sure your brother doesn't find out what it is, I've taken the precaution of concealing the secret ingredient's name in..."

Quiz 12: The Tough-ee Toffee Challenge

The secret ingredient that will seal your brother's lips for ever and the other nine ingredients you might (or might not) consider putting into a special toffee recipe for your brother are all hidden either <u>across</u> or <u>down</u> in the word-search quiz below.

X	Q	W	T	E	E	H	O	O	T
F	Z	C	R	I	H	A	L	L	O
R	S	O	U	R	M	I	L	K	F
O	O	G	E	P	M	R	S	U	F
G	S	U	P	E	R	G	L	U	E
S	L	N	V	C	H	E	E	S	E
P	I	G	S	W	I	L	L	M	N
A	M	E	H	E	L	P	U	Y	T
W	E	L	L	Y	U	M	M	Y	Y
N	P	O	T	N	O	O	D	L	E

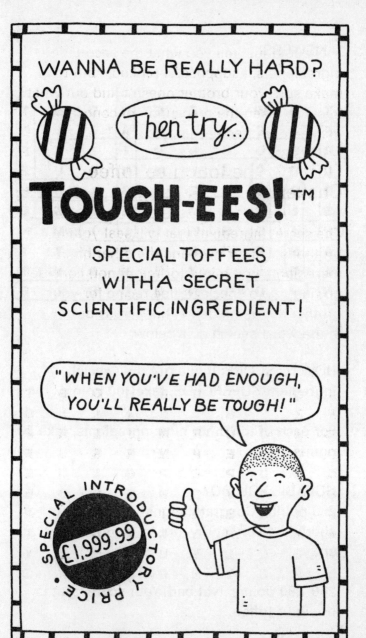

ANSWERS:

X	Q	W	T	E	E	H	O	O	T
F	Z	C	R	I	H	A	L	L	O
R	S	O	U	R	M	I	L	K	F
O	O	G	E	P	M	R	S	U	F
G	S	U	P	E	R	G	L	U	E
S	L	N	V	C	H	E	E	S	E
P	I	G	S	W	I	L	L	M	N
A	M	E	H	E	L	P	U	Y	T
W	E	L	L	Y	U	M	M	Y	Y
N	P	O	T	N	O	O	D	L	E

HOW TO SCORE: If you got the special ingredient SUPERGLUE, take 100 points.

For each of the other nine ingredients, take 20 points.

HOW DID YOU DO?
280 points: Congratulations! Your toffee should be very sticky, not to mention very sicky.

200–280 points: Not bad! Your score, that is, not your toffee.

Less than 200 points: Good effort! When you're doing quizzes with glue in them, it's very easy to get stuck.

Now enter your score from Quiz 12 on your How To Handle Your Family Ultimate Quiz Score Chart on page 107 at the back of the book.

Quiz 13: Have You A Clue-Dohh Who Did It?

The How To Handle Your Family Clue-Dohh Game will help give you an idea of some of the stuff your brother gets up to. It's like Cluedo, but because your brother is likely to be a bit dozy, it's been renamed Clue-dohh.

Below is a list of crimes that have taken place over the last few days. All you have to do is simply solve who did them.

HOW TO SCORE: take 10 points for every crime correctly solved!

CRIME NO 1.
Someone has absolutely murdered your fave
Nuclear Puppydogs CD. Was it:

A) MRS TWITTY
the cook with a
bloodstained meat
cleaver?

B) REV NERDY
the vicar with an
automatic sub-
machine gun?

C) YOUR BROTHER
with his clumsy,
fat fingers?

CRIME NO 2.
Someone has got thick red stains all over
your new jacket! Was it:

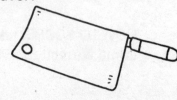

A) LADY BURP the
twerp with a
bloodstained meat
cleaver?

B) OLD HEAP the gardener with a bloodstained Lady Burp the twerp?

C) YOUR BROTHER with the tomato ketchup?

CRIME NO 3.

Someone has punctured the life out of your brand-new World Cup football! Was it:

A) MRS TWITTY the cook with a bloodstained automatic sub-machine gun?

B) OLD HEAP the gardener with a bloodstained automatic sub-machine Flymo?

C) YOUR BROTHER with a set of Dracula fangs from the joke-shop?

CRIME NO 4.
Someone has poisoned your dinner. Was it:

A) OLD BOOTS the chemist with a bottle of arsenic?

B) COLONEL KEN TUCKY with his fried chicken?

C) YOUR BROTHER with a jar of frogspawn?

CRIME NO 5.
Someone has sealed your brother's lips up! Was it:

A) MR MACKNIFE the surgeon with a needle and thread?

B) MR PRITT with his little stick?

C) YOU with a bag of toffees?

ANSWERS:
CRIME NO 1. Answer C
CRIME NO 2. Answer C
CRIME NO 3. Answer C
CRIME NO 4. Answer C
CRIME NO 5. Answer C

HOW DID YOU SCORE?
50 points: Well done! You're quite the detective! Pleased to meet you, Chief Inspector Quite!

30–40 points: Not bad! I guess you're a bit of a SLEUTH!

20 points or less: Need some work here. I guess you're a bit of a SLOTH!

*Now enter your score from Quiz 13
on your How To Handle Your Family
Ultimate Quiz Score Chart on page
108 at the back of the book.*

"Thanks, Quizmister," said Tanya. "I'll never look at my brother in quite the same light again."

"You'd save yourself a lot of pain if you didn't look at him at all," I replied. "Now, I guess it's time we turned to..."

Handling Super-Sisters

A look of agony spread across Talinder's face. Probably because I was standing on his toes at the time.

"So," I said, "pencils at the ready for..."

Quiz 14: What Sort Of Super-Sister Have You Got?

Put a ring round the answers which best describe what your sister is like:

QUESTIONS: ANSWERS:

1. Which of these foods is your sister most like?

A) Stir fry
B) Sponge
C) Dhal

2. What is your
sister's fave book?

A) Spot the dog
B) Spot the ball
C) Spot the spot

3. What is your
sister's fave sport?

A) Horse racing
B) Hose racing
C) Water sports

4. Which of these
pets is your sister
most like?

A) Bunny the rabbit
B) Kitty the cat
C) Willy the
wildebeest

5. Who is the
scariest?

A) Cruella de Vil
B) The Wicked Witch
of the West
C) Your sister

Now add up your sister's scores like this:

1. A) 5 points – it doesn't matter if they're big
fry or small fry, all sisters are stirrers.
B) 10 points – your sister's always trying to
sponge stuff off you – CDs, games, sweets…
And I bet at tea time, she even tries to sponge
sponge off you.
C) 100 points – I know, your sister never stops
dhalling on her mobile phone. Texting her
mates, chatting to them…

2. A) 5 points – this is a harmless little picture
book about a lovable puppy called Spot. OK if
your sister's aged about three, but if she's any
older she really ought to be reading more
advanced cuddly animal stories – like *Revenge
of the Well-Scary Werewolf* or *Kevin the Killer
Dog Goes to the Park*?
B) 10 points – this is obviously a harmless
little picture book about a lovable *football*
called Spot. Sad or what?
C) 100 points – no surprise here; your sister's
reading a book about looking for zits.

3. A) 5 points – sisters just love horses. No
wonder so many of them look like them.
B) 10 points – this mean sport involves your
sister racing after you with the garden hose.

Probably because you told her she had a face like a horse. I mean, has she *no* sense of humour?
C) 100 points – unfortunately this means *drenching* you with the hose.

4. A) 5 points – OK, your sister may not exactly look like a cuddly bunny, but I bet she rabbits on and on and on...
B) 10 points – your sister's a bit of a sour puss.
C) 100 points – so, your sister is either really wilde, or a beest or both.

5. A) 0 points – OK, she might scare you if you were a dog with spots. But I doubt that she'd even scare a sister with spots.
B) 0 points – Not to be confused with your sister in her athletics kit: The Wicked Witch of the Vest.

C) 100 points!

WHAT THE SCORES MEAN:
If your sister has scored up to 30 points she's
a NICE MAIDEN. This is virtually unheard of,
so ring the *Guinness Book of Records*
immediately!

30–100 points: She's an ICE MAIDEN.

Over 100 points: She's an ICE CREAM or more
likely an ICE SCREAM.

> *Now enter your sister's score from Quiz
> 14, together with the name of the type
> of sister you now know you have, on
> your How To Handle Your Family Dead
> Important Family Factfinder File on
> page 106 at the back of this book.*

"Right," said Talinder, "Now perhaps you'll tell
me how I can get my sister
out of the best bedroom in
our chalet?"

"She's not bagged the
best bedroom for
herself?" I asked.
"I can't believe
she'd do such
a despicable
thing."

"Come and look for yourself," said Talinder. And so we did.

There was Talinder's sister in the best bedroom in their chalet!

"*You* should have the best room in the holiday chalet," Tony told Talinder.

"Yes," agreed Tamara. "It's your right. Or rather it's *on your right*. As you go in the front door."

"Don't worry. I have a solution," I said. "What you've got to do is make your sister believe that the best room in the chalet is haunted! She'll get out of it soon enough then, leaving it free for you to move into!"

woooooooo !

"Great! But what sort of things are most likely to scare Talinder's sister out of her wits?" asked Tom.

"Yes... I'm not even sure she's got any," pointed out Talinder.

So I told them, "All is explained in Quiz 15, which is like your brother's nose after you've finished with it: ie, in three parts..."

Quiz 15 Part A: How To Tell A Great Big Scary From A Great Big Fairy

Below is a list of stuff that is likely to scare your sister. Unfortunately, I was a bit tired when I put them together and the gruesome pictures have been labelled wrongly. Match the right gruesome picture to the right grisly label.

HOW TO SCORE: Take 10 points for each answer you get right.

1. FEARSOME FACES

i)   ii)  iii)

A) A ghoul's face   B) Quasimodo's face   C) A girl's face

2. CREEPY CRAWLIES

i)  ii)   iii)

A) A louse   B) A spider   C) A woodlouse

3. BOTHERSOME BEASTIES

i)

ii)

iii)

A) Mousse   B) Mouse   C) Moose

4. HIDEOUS HOWLS

i)

ii)

iii)

A) The
Squidgy
Bogies'
latest CD

B) Banshees
moaning

C) Wails of
the undead

5. SCARIEST SENSATIONS

i)

ii)

iii)

A) A hug
from your
gran*

B) A brush
across your
cheek from a
vampire bat

C) The grasp
of a haunted
hand

* See the GRAN section on pages 52–69.

ANSWERS:
1. i) = C)
   ii) = A)
   iii) = B)

2. i) = B)
   ii) = C)
   iii) = A)

3. i) = B)
   ii) = C)
   iii) = A)

4. i) = B)
   ii) = C)
   iii) = A)

5. i) = C)
   ii) = A)
   iii) = B)

HOW DID YOU SCORE?
150 points: Well done! You're the ghostest with the mostest!

50–150 points: Not bad! You're getting there – into the best bedroom in the holiday chalet, that is.

Less than 50 points: You really are a pot of strawberry mousse (see page 92); ie, you don't scare me and I bet you don't scare your sister either.

Now enter your score from Quiz 15 Part A on your How To Handle Your Family Ultimate Quiz Score Chart on page 108 at the back of the book.

"Right," I explained to Talinder and the others. "Now that you've got the pictures sorted out with their proper labels, all you've got to do is to work out which you think is most likely to scare your sister out of her wits and out of the best bedroom in the chalet. In other words, all you've got to do is..."

Quiz 15 Part B: Scaredy Cat-egories

HOW TO SCORE: Take 10 points for each answer you get right.

WHICH OF THE FOLLOWING IS MOST LIKELY TO SCARE YOUR SISTER?

1. FACES

A) The face of a hideous ghoul

B) The face of a hideous girl

C) The face of Quasimodo

2. CREEPY CRAWLIES

A) A louse   B) A spider   C) A woodlouse

3. BOTHERSOME BEASTIES

A) A mousse   B) A mouse   C) A moose

4. HIDEOUS HOWLS

A) The Squidgy   B) Banshees   C) Wails of
Bogies' latest CD   moaning   the undead

5. SCARIEST SENSATIONS

A) A hug from   B) A brush   C) The grasp
your gran   across your   of a
                  cheeks from   haunted
                  a vampire bat   hand

ANSWERS:

1. FACES

A) Yes – the one that will really scare your sister!

B) No. Your sister looks in the mirror at least 156 times a day and it doesn't seem to scare her one little bit.

C) No. Quasimodo's likely to remind her of the lad she meets down at the karaoke bar.

2. CREEPY CRAWLIES

A) Yes – the one that will really scare your sister! Your brother – the little louse – is enough to scare anyone.

B) No – unless your sister's name is Muffet and she's just gone and sat herself down on a tuffet, whatever that is.

C) No – unlikely to scare your sister. She probably crunches them up live between her teeth to exercise her jaw muscles. Think of it not so much as a woodlouse as a wouldn't louse.

3. BOTHERSOME BEASTIES

A) No – unless it's styling mousse on your dad's hair. Well scary!

B) Yes – the one that will really scare your sister! For added effect place a sign saying "I'M REALLY A RAT" around the mouse's neck.

C) No – your sister's likely to turn to the moose and say, "Oh, you are a deer!"

4. HIDEOUS HOWLS

A) Yes – the one that will really scare your sister!

B) No. Compared to the Squidgy Bogies latest CD the sound of banshees moaning is about as scary as the sound of your mum moaning.

C) No. Compared to the Squidgy Bogies' latest CD these sound about as scary as the Tweenies.

5. SCARIEST SENSATIONS

A: Yes – the one that will really scare your sister!

B: No. Compared with a hug from your gran, a vampire brush is about as scary as a Basil Brush.

C: No. Anyone who's held hands with Lenny Lickspittle (like your sister has) isn't going to be scared by this!

HOW DID YOU SCORE?

50 points: Well done! Not only are you the ghostest with the mostest, you're a pretty cool ghoul, too!

30–40 points: Not bad! Unlike Lenny Lickspittle (see C on page 98) who is. Bad, that is. Very.

Less than 30 points: Dreadful! You must feel like a bit of filleted fish: ie, totally gutted.

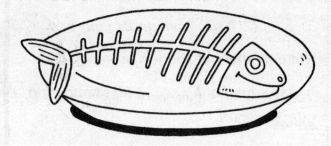

Now enter your score from Quiz 15 Part B on your How To Handle Your Family Ultimate Quiz Score Chart on page 108 at the back of the book.

"Finally," I said, "now you know just what is going to scare your sister, you can send her the following letter. Just fill in the missing words from Part B."

Quiz 15 Part C: Missing Words

My dearest ....*

I am writing to tell you that the best

bedroom in the holiday chalet that you

have bagged for yourself is haunted. Late

at night the face of a dreadful ....(1)

appears at the window and a horrible little

...........(2) hides itself under your bed.

Not only that but you will be kept awake

by the sound of a ....(3) scampering

about.

And if that isn't bad enough, the

sound of the ....(4) Bogies will echo

through the walls** and you will be visited

by ....(5) coming in to give you a

goodnight ....(6) Terrifying, or what?

* Enter your sister's name here.
**ie, as you switch on the CD player in your room.

That is why I implore you to get out of that bedroom as soon as you can, taking your Beanie Babies, Top Hits magazines and broomstick with you (but leaving your top-secret, very personal diary).

Your ever loving

brother/sister/gran*

....**

---

* Delete as necessary. And if you are a gran reading this – stop immediately and give this book back to the person it belongs to. Thank you.

** Sign your name here.

ANSWERS:
1. ghoul
2. louse
3. mouse
4. Squidgy
5. Gran
6. hug

HOW DID YOU SCORE?
There's only one way to score this quiz:

Did you scare your sister out of her wits?

YES?

NO?

Take 100 points
(and the best bedroom
in the chalet!)

Take my deepest
sympathy. Your
sister is obviously
completely
unscareable,
probably because
she's a bit of a
ghoul herself.

As soon as Talinder's sister got his letter, she
was out of the best bedroom like a shot.

Tamara, Tom, Tanya, Tony and I left him moving his stuff in and wandered back in the direction of my chalet.

"That family-handling activity course was brilliant, Quizmister," said Tamara.

"I know," I agreed, modestly.

"You should write a book about it," said Tom.

"Do you think so?" I asked.

"Yes," said Tony. "I bet it'd be really good."

"Of course it would," I agreed, modestly, of course.

"And it'd make you rich and famous," added Tanya.

"Really?" I said.

"Oh yes," they all said.

I went back into my chalet and thought long and hard. Then I thought short and soft. I booted up my computer...

...and wrote:

It was a bright and sunny day and the little baa-lambs were frolicking in the field...

Then I deleted it and wrote:

It was a dark and stormy night...

THE HOW TO HANDLE YOUR FAMILY DEAD IMPORTANT FAMILY FACTFINDER FILE

FROM QUIZ 1 (page 16)
My mum's score was: ....

The kind of mum I've got:

....

FROM QUIZ 3 (page 29)
The special Super-Mum Crossword is:

....

FROM QUIZ 4 (page 35)
My dad's score was: ....

The kind of dad I've got:

....

FROM QUIZ 6 (page 49)
The Super-Dad-Speak phrase is:

....

FROM QUIZ 8 (page 54)
The year my gran was born: ....

The kind I've gran I've got:

....

FROM QUIZ 11 (page 70)
My brother's score was: ....

The kind of brother I've got:

....

FROM QUIZ 14 (page 85)
My sister's score was: ....

The kind of sister I've got:

....

THE HOW TO HANDLE YOUR FAMILY ULTIMATE QUIZ SCORE CHART

MY SCORE

FROM QUIZ 2 (page 24): ....

FROM QUIZ 5 (page 43): ....

FROM QUIZ 7 (page 53): ....

FROM QUIZ 9 (page 62): ....

FROM QUIZ 10 (page 66): ....

FROM QUIZ 12 (page 76): ....

FROM QUIZ 13 (page 79): ....

FROM QUIZ 15:

Part A (page 91): ....

Part B (page 95): ....

Part C (page 100): ....

MY TOTAL ULTIMATE HOW TO HANDLE YOUR FAMILY SCORE IS:

....

WHAT YOUR ULTIMATE QUIZ SCORE MEANS:

Over 750 points: Congratulations! You have achieved the Award of Family Handler Grade One (1st Class)

Between 250 and 750 points: Well done! You have achieved the award of Family Handler Grade One and a Half (376th Class)

Less than 250 points: Come on! Even your dad could do better than this. You have achieved the award of Family Handler Grade Minus One and a Half and I'm afraid you have no class at all.

Your unique How To Handle Your Family Handler's Certificate is on the next page. Just fill in your Grade and Class.

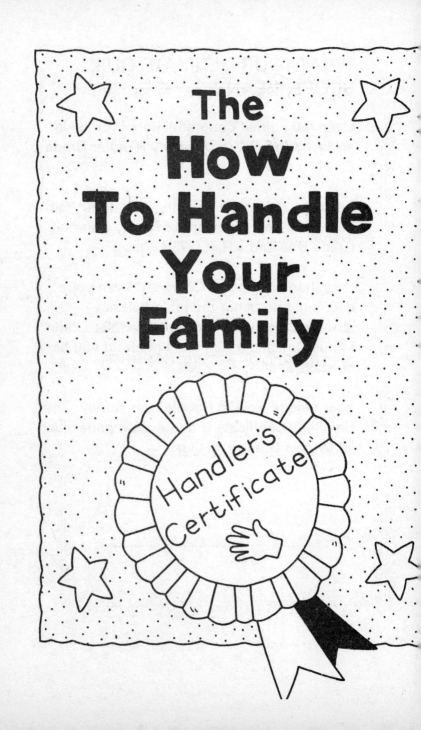

This is to certify that

Name...

has achieved the following
in the art of family handling

Grade...

Class...